The Football Maths Book
The World Cup

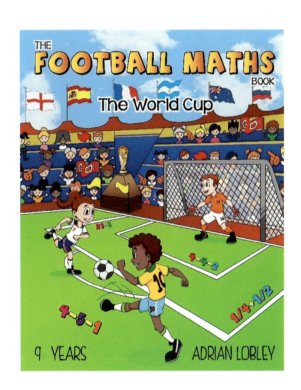

Adrian Lobley

To Sebastian

With thanks to:
Sebastian Wraith-Lobley
Sarah Wraith
Logan Nicholson
Kaden Nicholson
Callan Nicholson
Asher Nicholson
Derry Nicholson
Andrea Nicholson
Miss O'Donnell
Miss Town
Finlay Cronshaw

Front/back cover illustrations by:
Alyssa Josue

Copyright © 2018 Adrian Lobley
All rights reserved.
ISBN-13: 978-1983447426
ISBN-10: 1983447420

 A 2D shape is **symmetrical** if a line can be drawn through it so that either side of the line looks exactly the same. This is the line of **symmetry**.

Here are flags of 4 countries (the years each country hosted the World Cup are shown). Draw a line of symmetry on ONLY the flags that are symmetrical (in both **colour** and **shape**). The first one has been done for you (see the red line on Sweden's flag).

Sweden (1958)   Brazil (1950, 2014)   Japan (2002)   South Africa (2010)

The following countries have all won the World Cup (the years they won it are shown). For those flags that are symmetrical, draw the line of symmetry on them.

France (1998)   Spain (2010)   Italy (1934, 1938, 2006)   Uruguay (1930, 1950)

The flags below have either 1 or 2 lines of symmetry. Draw on their lines of symmetry.

Holland   England   Scotland   Russia

Did you know: The first World Cup was in 1930. Also the World Cups in 1942 and 1946 were cancelled due to World War II.

Circle the odd number out on the football shirts below.

8   4   14   6   (3)   10

Why is it the odd one out?   because its odd ✓

Can you spot the odd one out here?

10   25   (12)   20   30   35

Why is it the odd one out?   because its not in the 5 times table ✓

Can you spot the odd one out here?

12   3   9   15   (4)   18

Why is it the odd one out?   Its not in the 3 times table ✓

2

The footballs below cost the same amount.

 + = £2   How much does each football cost?  1 pound ✓

The football shirts below cost the same amount

 + + = £6   How much does each shirt cost? 2 pounds ✓

Using the 2 answers above, work out how much the following cost…

 + = 3 pounds ✓

 + + = £30   How much does each trophy cost?  10 pounds ✓

 + + = £15   How much does each football cost? 5 pounds ✓

Using the 2 answers above, work out how much the following cost…

 + = 15 pounds ✓

3

**Multiples of 6 include:
6, 12, 18, 24, 30, 36, 42, 48**

Start at the bottom of the grid below and draw a route to goal (moving vertically (up or down) or horizontally (left to right or right to left)) using **multiples of 6**.

Below is an example:

18	26	8	30
12	24	6	24
18	14	18	12
6	4	44	11

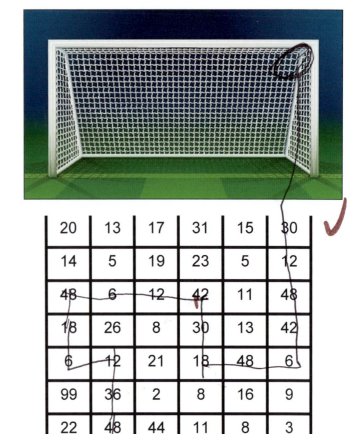

20	13	17	31	15	30
14	5	19	23	5	12
48	6	12	42	11	48
18	26	8	30	13	42
6	12	21	18	48	6
99	36	2	8	16	9
22	48	44	11	8	3

4

Roman numerals originated in ancient Rome and remained the usual way of writing numbers throughout Europe, well into the Middle Ages

Look at the table below. You can see that when the Romans wanted to use the number 6, they wrote VI. When they wanted to use the number 50, they wrote 'L'.

Numbers	1	2	3	4	5	6	7	8	9	10	50	100	500	1000
Roman Numerals	I	II	III	IV	V	VI	VII	VIII	IX	X	L	C	D	M

Use the table to calculate the sums below and write the answers in Roman numerals:

X + X + X + X + X = [XL] ✓

I + VIII + I = [X] ✓

L ÷ X = [V] ✓

Former Serbian defender Nemanja Vidic played for clubs including Manchester Utd and Inter Milan.

His surname 'VIDIC' is made up of Roman Numerals. Sums have been created below using the letters of his surname. Write the answers using normal numbers, not Roman Numerals.

V + I + D + I + C = [scribbled out]

V - I + D - I - C = [scribbled out]

403 I can not read.

5

Before the World Cup in the USA in 1994, teams got **2** points if they won a match. From 1994 onwards teams got **3** points for a win.

1) The following countries got the results below **before 1994, when it was 2 points for a Win**. Calculate their points and circle the country with the most points.

W=Win
D=Draw (**1** point)
L=Loss (**0** points)

Team	Results					Points
Serbia	W	D	L	D	D	
Mexico	W	L	W	L	L	

2) If these teams had got the identical results **after 1994** which team would have the most points?
Hint: This time it is 3 points for a win because it is after 1994, so every 'W'=3 points

Team	Results					Points
Serbia	W	D	L	D	D	
Mexico	W	L	W	L	L	

3) In the future, if it becomes 4 points for a win, how many points do the teams get below?
Hint: Every 'W' =4 points

Team	Results					Points
Serbia	W	D	L	D	D	
Mexico	W	L	W	L	L	

Did you notice that the results in all 3 tables are identical? Yet Serbia got more points than Mexico when it was 2 points for a win (1st table) but less points when it was 4 points for a win (3rd table).

Below are 4 World Cup football groups. The number next to each country is that country's world ranking. So you can see that Brazil are ranked Number 1 in the world.

GROUP A
Team
Brazil (1)
Croatia (11)
Mexico (4)
Cameroon (16)

GROUP B
Team
Spain (2)
Russia (10)
Greece (12)
Holland (3)

GROUP C
Team
Columbia (14)
Chile (9)
Ivory Coast (8)
Japan (13)

GROUP D
Team
Uruguay (7)
Costa Rica (15)
England (6)
Italy (5)

Which is the lowest ranked country out of all the teams above? ☐

Have a guess which group has the best teams in overall. ☐

Can you think of a way to work out which group is **actually** the best - by using the ranking numbers?

Hint: An empty row has been added under each group, for you to write in. Use this to add up the rankings in each group eg Brazil + Croatia + Mexico + Cameroon = 1+11+4+16

So, mathematically, which is the best group? ☐

Hint: Have a think about whether the toughest group is the one with the highest total or the one with the lowest total.

7

Below, legendary goalscorer *Stephen Stephenson* heads the ball at the only square in the goal that is a **Prime Number**. Which square does he head the ball at? *(Hint: Prime Numbers are explained below)*

 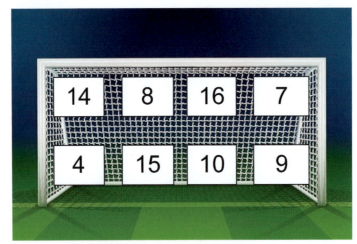

A **Prime Number** can only be divided by 1 or itself. It must be a whole number that is a greater than 1.

So '5' is a Prime Number because it can only be divided evenly by 1 or 5.

'6' can be divided evenly by 1 and 6. However, as it can be divided by something else eg 2 and 3, this means it is NOT a prime number.

The number 7 is an example of a Prime Number because it can only be divided by 1 and 7 (itself).
It can't be divided by eg 2,3,4,5 or 6

Start at the bottom of the grid and draw a route to goal using only **Prime Numbers**.

20	13	14	30	15	40
14	5	7	19	11	5
48	6	12	42	18	17
18	26	8	30	13	11
6	12	24	19	7	6
99	11	3	13	16	9
22	7	44	6	8	4

9

- Below, 1 defender, 1 midfielder and 1 striker touch the ball before scoring.
- The numbers on the back of those 3 players' shirts add up to the number in the goal.
- Which defender, midfielder and striker touch the ball in each puzzle?

The first puzzle has been done for you.
Example: 6+4+10=20

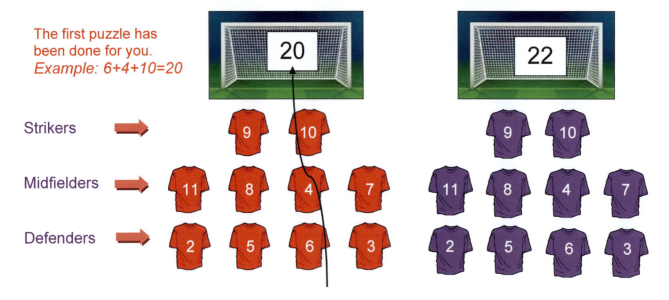

In the puzzles below, **4 players** touch the ball: 1 Defender, **2 midfielders** and 1 striker. Which 4 players touch the ball?

The ball can only be passed horizontally or vertically to the player next to or in front.

3 players were involved in scoring a goal. To find out which 3, you have to add 3 player's shirt numbers so that it equals the number in the goal.

Draw a circle around the player's shirts who were involved in the goal.

Which **3 players** were involved in this goal?

For this next game, **4 players** are involved in the goal. Circle the correct **4**.

For the final game, **4 players** are involved in the goal. Circle the correct **4**.

11

Italy have 3 colours in their flag: Green White Red

Russia have 3 colours in their flag: White Blue Red

Did you notice that Italy and Russia both have White and Red in their flags? Let's combine Italy's oval shape and Russia's oval shape. We write 'White and Red' just once in the area where the ovals overlap. We call this a **Venn diagram**.

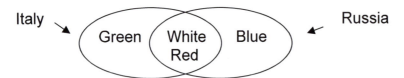

There is a World Cup match between Costa Rica and Columbia:
Both flags share Blue and Red. Write in the missing colours in the Venn diagram

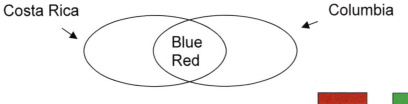

There is a World Cup match between Holland and Ireland:

Write in the colours in the Venn diagram. Remember, if a colour appears in both flags, just write it in once, in the middle section.

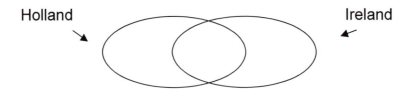

12

Each team below has played 1 match against 1 of the other teams in the group.

GROUP A	Played	Won	Drawn	Lost	For	Against
Brazil	1	1	0	0	3	0
Croatia	1	0	1	0	1	1
Mexico	1	0	1	0	1	1
Cameroon	1	0	0	1	0	3

Which team won a match? [____]   What score did they win by? [__] - [__]

Hint: 'For' = Number of goals they scored.   'Against' = Number of goals they let in

Who did Brazil play against? [____]

Hint: The score of the team Brazil played against must have been the opposite of 3-0.

Write in the teams and score in the other match _____ [__] - [__] _____

---

1 more match gets played between 2 of the teams. From the table below can you work out which 2 teams played and what the score was?
Hint: Brazil won their first match above 3-0. Below you can see they have played another match (see 'Played'=2) and they have scored 5 goals in total in the 2 matches (because 'For'=5) and haven't conceded any in the 2 matches (because 'Against'=0)

GROUP A	Played	Won	Drawn	Lost	For	Against
Brazil	2	2	0	0	5	0
Croatia	1	0	1	0	1	1
Mexico	2	0	1	1	1	3
Cameroon	1	0	0	1	0	3

_____ [__] - [__] _____

13

In Group B, 1 World Cup match has been played. The score was: **Germany 4-3 Portugal**
The league table now looks like this:

GROUP B	Played	Won	Drawn	Lost	For	Against
Germany	1	1	0	0	4	3
Russia	0	0	0	0	0	0
Japan	0	0	0	0	0	0
Portugal	1	0	0	1	3	4

The next match result was: **Russia 2-2 Japan**. Complete the league table below.
Hint: 'For' = The total number of goals a team has scored. 'Against' = The total number of goals a team has conceded

GROUP B	Played	Won	Drawn	Lost	For	Against
Germany	1	1	0	0	4	3
Russia						
Japan						
Portugal	1	0	0	1	3	4

2 more matches were then played in this group and the table now looks like this:

GROUP A	Played	Won	Drawn	Lost	For	Against
Germany	2	2	0	0	6	3
Russia	2	0	2	0	3	3
Japan	2	0	1	1	2	4
Portugal	2	0	1	1	4	5

At the top of the page Germany won their first match 4-3. After 2 matches they have scored 6 in total and conceded 3 in total (see the green squares above). So what was the score in their second match?

☐ - ☐

You're the new manager of your country! Your squad includes: **5 defenders, 5 midfielders, 5 attackers**. You will need to pick any 10 of these players on a matchday.

If every player was available, then you could choose any one of many formations
 eg: 5-3-2, 4-4-2 etc ('5-3-2' means: 5 Defenders, 3 midfielders and 2 attackers).

However in the next 3 matches you have lots of injuries and suspensions so you have a smaller number of players available to choose from.

Match 1: 11 out of 15 players are available: **4 defenders, 4 midfielders, 3 attackers**
Can you work out the 3 formations you could use? One has been done for you…

Using 4 defenders: | 4 - 3 - 3 | | *Hint: It needs to add up to 10*

Using 3 defenders: | |

Match 2: 11 out of 15 players are available: **4 defenders, 5 midfielders, 2 attackers**
Can you work out the 3 formations you could use?

Using 4 defenders: | | |

Using 3 defenders: | |

Match 3: 12 out of 15 players are available: **4 defenders, 5 midfielders, 3 attackers**
Can you work out the 6 formations you could use?

Using 4 defenders: | | | |

Using 3 defenders: | | |

Using 2 defenders | |

15

In the puzzle below the goalkeeper has kicked the ball to the Number 4. We know this because we have added 1 + 3 = 4. Work out the number of the player who received the ball next. Write this on the shirt. Then do the last calculation to find out who scored the goal.

Try another one. Which number player scored this time…

You're the manager of a 5-a-side football team. Write 4 of your friend's names here:

1 <u>Hall</u> 2 _____ 3 _____ 4 _____ 5 _____

Write in the names of the players on the shirts below to see which friend scored.

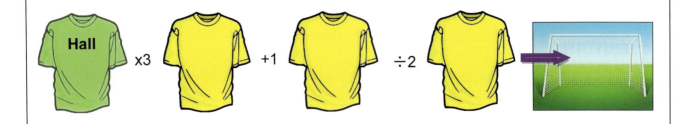

Multiples of 6 include:
36, 42, 48, 54, 60, 66, 72

Start at the bottom of the grid below and draw a route to goal (moving vertically or horizontally) using **multiples of 6**.

51	13	60	31	15	35
48	54	42	23	5	11
42	66	10	41	11	46
48	17	54	72	54	60
36	72	42	19	41	36
99	35	49	8	42	72
22	47	44	11	66	32

Each team below has played 1 match against 1 of the other teams in the group.

GROUP A	Played	Won	Drawn	Lost	For	Against
China	1	1	0	0	4	0
Sweden	1	1	0	0	2	0
Estonia	1	0	0	1	0	2
Jamaica	1	0	0	1	0	4

1 result is below. From the info in the table, work out the other result and enter below

Match 1: China 4-0 Jamaica   **Match 2:** _____

After the above matches, China then play Estonia, and Sweden play Jamaica. Following these 2 new matches the league table has been updated (below). Work out the 2 match scores from the table and enter them in the boxes below.

GROUP A	Played	Won	Drawn	Lost	For	Against
China	2	1	1	0	6	2
Sweden	2	1	1	0	3	1
Estonia	2	0	1	1	2	4
Jamaica	2	0	1	1	1	5

China [ ] - [ ] **Estonia**   **Sweden** [ ] - [ ] **Jamaica**

Hint: China won their first match 4-0 (at the top of the page). The 2nd table shows that China have now drawn a match. It also shows that they have now scored a total of 6 goals (see the red 'For' square) and they have now conceded a total of 2 goals (see the red 'Against' square). So they must have drawn their 2nd match 2-2. Now use the same technique to find out Sweden's result (look at the yellow squares).

18

In 1975, England striker Malcolm MacDonald (whose nickname was 'SuperMac') scored 5 goals in 1 match! The score was:

England 5-0 Cyprus (MACDONALD 5)

5 of the letters in MACDONALD are Roman Numerals. Here's the Roman numeral table.

| Roman Numerals | I | II | III | IV | V | VI | VII | VIII | IX | X | L | C | D | M |

Go through each letter in the name MACDONALD and if it is a Roman numeral, write it in a box below. The first one has been done for you:

| M | | | | |

Here is the table showing the numeric values of Roman Numerals eg M=1000

Numbers	1	2	3	4	5	6	7	8	9	10	50	100	500	1000
Roman Numerals	I	II	III	IV	V	VI	VII	VIII	IX	X	L	C	D	M

Now translate the Roman Numerals that appear in the name MACDONALD, into numbers

| 1000 | | | | |

CHALLENGE QUESTION: What number do you get if you add these up? | |

Hint: First add up the M, then add up the 2 D's, then the others.

Did you know, Romans used to play a similar game to football called "Harpastum" although they were allowed to use their hands as well as their feet.

19

This football game is about finding out how many goals each player has scored in a season. Look at the pyramid of 3 boxes below.

Striker ➡
Midfielders ➡

So one midfielder scored 5 goals and the other has scored 3 goals. **In these puzzles, the box above always adds up to the total of the 2 boxes below**. So the striker scored as many goals as the 2 midfielders, added together. Write in the top box the number of goals the striker scored.

In another team, here are the number of goals scored by a midfielder and a striker.

Striker ➡
Midfielders ➡
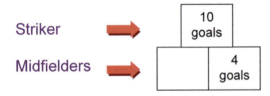

The box above always adds up to the total of the 2 boxes below it. Write in the number of goals the other midfielder scored.

In another team, 5 players have scored goals. What numbers go in the blank boxes?

Striker ➡
Midfielders ➡
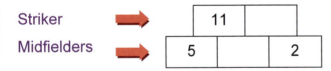

Hint: Each time, try to look for a pyramid of 3 boxes, where you have 2 of the numbers:

Then....

20

In another team, some defenders have scored too. See the pyramid below. **Can you work out how many goals the other midfielder scored?** Write your answer in this box.

Striker → | | 10 | |
Midfielders → | 6 | | |
Defenders → | | | 2 |

Now, can you now work out the number of goals the middle defender has scored?
Hint: Just use the 3 boxes to work this out ie the one you have just written in and the one with the number 2 in it.

Can you now work out how many goals the final defender scored?

In another team, 9 different players scored this season. How many did each score?

Strikers → | 16 | | |
Midfielders → | | 3 | |
Defenders → | 2 | | 1 |

Complete the boxes to find out who scored the most goals in this team

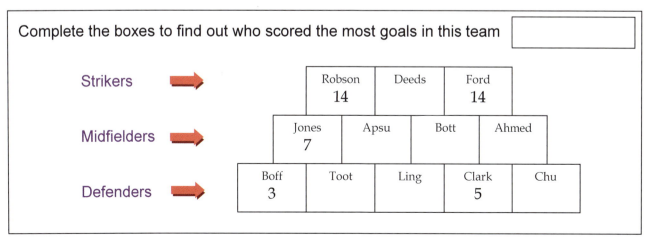

21

2 players were involved in scoring a goal. To find out which 2, you have to **multiply** 2 player's shirt numbers so that it equals the number in the goal.

Draw a circle around the player's shirts who were involved in the goal.

Which 2 players were involved in this one (ie which 2 numbers do you need to **multiply**).

For this next game, **3 players** are involved in the goal. Circle the correct **3**.

Hint: 2 of the answers are: '3' and '4'. So multiply 3 and 4. Now what do you need to multiply that answer by, to get to 60? Is it 5 or 10? Circle the 3 numbers used, above.

For the final game, **3 players** are involved in the goal. Circle the correct **3**.

Have you ever played 'Spot the ball'? 'Spot the ball' is where there is a picture of a player kicking a ball but the ball has been removed. You have to guess where the ball was.

This puzzle is similar. You have to work out which number the football is hidden behind…

37	38	39	40
33	34	35	36
29	30	31	32
25	26	27	28
21	22	23	24
17	18	19	20
13	14	15	16
9	10	11	12
5	6	7	8
1	2	3	4

Use these clues to find out…

- It doesn't have a 3 in the number (Hint: Cross out all numbers containing a 3 eg 34)

- It's a prime number (Hint: Cross out all the numbers which are not prime numbers eg 8)

- The number is > 19 (Hint: '>' means 'Greater than')

- The number is < 36 (Hint: '<' means 'Less than')

Write the number here that is hiding the ball

23

1) This puzzle is about Time. Use a pencil to draw a route from the top goal to the bottom goal. You can only move horizontally or vertically. The time begins at 8:30 in the top goal. To get to the bottom (12:00) you have to move to a square which is 15 minutes later than the square you are on. So if you are on a square that is 9:15, then you need to draw a line to one that says 9:30.

	8:30		
6:30	8:00	8:45	9:00
7:45	7:30	9:30	9:15
8:15	9:00	9:45	10:00
11:00	10:45	10:30	10:15
11:15	10:00	8:45	10:00
11:30	11:45	7:15	9:30
	12:00		

2) In this puzzle use a pencil to find the route from the top of the goal to the bottom. To find out which squares to move though, work through the list on the left. The first one is 'Half past 7' which is the same as 7:30. So you begin at 7:30. The next one in the list is 'A quarter to 10' which is 9:45. The next one in the list will always be touching the last one (ie horizontally or vertically).

- Half past 7
- A quarter to 10
- Half past 8
- A quarter past 10
- 11 O'clock
- A quarter past 11
- Half past 10
- A quarter to 10
- 10 O'clock
- A quarter to 12
- Noon

	7:30		
6:30	8:00	9:45	9:00
7:45	7:30	8:30	10:15
8:15	9:00	9:45	11:00
11:00	9:45	10:30	11:15
11:15	10:00	8:45	10:00
11:30	11:45	7:15	9:30

Below are some of the highest scoring matches in World Cup tournament history.

Year	Team	Score	Team	Match
1930	Argentina	6-3	Mexico	1
1938	Brazil	6-5	Poland	2
1954	Hungary	8-3	Germany	3
1954	Hungary	9-0	Korea Republic	4
1954	Germany	7-2	Turkey	5
1954	Austria	7-5	Switzerland	6
1958	France	7-3	Paraguay	7
1974	Yugoslavia	9-0	Zaire	8
1982	Hungary	10-1	El Salvador	9

Which team appears most in the table?

4 of the 9 matches were in 1 year. Which year?

Which team lost by 4 goals?

In which match did the winner score twice as many goals as their opponent?

How many matches finished with the victorious team winning by 9 goals?

Which match had the most goals scored in it (both teams added together)?

25

Answers

1) (a) Symmetrical flags: Sweden, Japan. Brazil isn't due to the blue globe & white line. South Africa isn't due to the red and blue sections   (b) France (horizontal line), Italy (horizontal line)   (c) Holland (horizonal line), England (2 lines, horizontal and vertical), Scotland (2 lines, horizontal and vertical), Russia (vertical line)

2) (a) 3 (it is the only odd number) (b) 12 (it's not a multiple of 5)   (c) 4 (it's not a multiple of 3)

3) (a) (i) £1, (ii) £2, (iii) £3   (b) (i) £10, (ii) £5, (iii) £15

4) 48, 36, 12, 6, 18, 48, 6, 12, 42, 30, 18, 48, 6, 42, 48, 12, 30

5) (a) L (b) X (c) V (d) 607 (e) 403

6) Table 1: 5, 4   Table 2: 6, 6   Table 3: 7, 8

7) Cameroon, B, B (Group A=28, Group B=27, Group C=44, Group D=33. Lowest is the best, ie B)

8) 7

9) 7, 11, 3, 13, 19, 7, 13, 11, 17, 5, 11, 19, 7, 5, 13

10) (a) 6,4,10   (b) 5,8,9   (c) 2,11,8,9   (d) 6,4,8,9 or 5,8,4,10

11) (a) 4,5,10 (b) 7,9,14 (c) 4,8.11.19 (d) 9,15,19,21

12) (a) Costa Rica=White, Columbia=Yellow   (b) Left: Red, Blue.   Middle: White.   Right: Green, Orange

13) (a) Brazil won 3-0 against Cameroon. The scond match was: Croatia 1-1 Mexico (b) Brazil 2-0 Mexico

14) (a) Russia: Played: 1, Won: 0, Drawn: 1, Lost: 0, For: 2, Against: 2   (b) Russia: Played: 1, Won: 0, Drawn: 1, Lost: 0, For: 2, Against: 2   (c) 2-0

15) Match 1: 4-3-3, 4-4-2, 3-4-3   Match 2: 4-5-1, 4-4-2, 3-5-2. Match 3: 4-5-1, 4-4-2, 4-3-3, 3-5-2, 3-4-3, 2-5-3

16) (a) No.3 scored (b) No.7 scored (c) Player No.2 scored

17) 66, 42, 72, 36, 60, 54, 72, 54, 42, 72, 36, 48, 42, 48, 54, 42, 60

18) (a) Sweden 2-0 Estonia (b) China 2-2 Estonia, Sweden 1-1 Jamaica

19) (a) MCDLD (b) 1000, 100, 500, 50, 500, (b) 2,150

20) (a) 8 (b) 6 (c) Midfielder = 6, Striker = 8

21) (a) Midfielder = 4, Defenders = 4 and 2 (b) Defenders = 11 and 1, Midfielders = 13 and 2, Striker = 5 (c) Deeds = 15

22) (a) 3x4=12 (b) 4x11=44 (c) 3x4x5=60 (d) 4x5x10=200

23) 29

24) (a) Hungary (b) 1954 (c) Paraguay (d) 3   (e) Austria 7-5 Switzerland

25) (a) 8:30, 8:45, 9:00, 9:15, 9:30, 9:45, 10:00, 10:15, 10:30, 10:45, 11:00, 11:15, 11:30, 11:45, 12:00

(b) 7:30, 9:45, 8:30, 10:15, 11:00, 11:15, 10:30, 9:45, 10:00, 11:45, 12:00

Books by Adrian Lobley

The Football Maths Book Series

Book 1: The Football Maths Book   (Age 4-7)
       The Soccer Math Book (US version)
       El libro de matemáticas de fútbol (Spanish version)
Book 2: The Football Maths Book   The Re-match! (Age 5-8)
Book 3: The Football Maths Book   The Christmas Match (Age 6-8)
Book 4: The Football Maths Book   The Birthday Party (Age 7-8)
Book 5: The Football Maths Book   The World Cup (Age 9)

    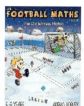  

The 'A Learn to Read Book' Series

A Learn to Read Book: The Football Match   (Ages 4-5)
A Learn to Read Book: The Tennis Match   (Ages 4-5)

 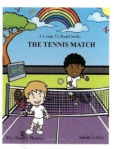

Children's Fiction

Kane and the Mystery of the Missing World Cup
Kane and the Christmas Football Adventure

For more information go to www.adrianlobley.com

Well don Jacob H
you tried your
best and I
like that. Alicia

shirt

ball

flag

goal

Printed in Great Britain
by Amazon